Relief without Cutting

Taking Your Negative Feelings
to God

Amy Baker

New
Growth
Press

www.newgrowthpress.com

New Growth Press, Greensboro, NC 27404
www.newgrowthpress.com
Copyright © 2011 by Amy Baker.
All rights reserved. Published 2011

Cover Design: Tandem Creative, Tom Temple,
tandemcreative.net

Typesetting: Lisa Parnell, lparnell.com

ISBN-10: 1-936768-36-4
ISBN-13: 978-1-936768-36-3

        Library of Congress Cataloging-in-Publication Data
Baker, Amy, 1959–
  Relief without cutting : taking your negative feelings to God /
Amy Baker.
      p. cm.
  Includes bibliographical references and index.
  ISBN-13: 978-1-936768-36-3 (alk. paper)
  ISBN-10: 1-936768-36-4 (alk. paper)
  1. Cutting (Self-mutilation)—Religious aspects—Christianity.
2. Emotions—Religious aspects—Christianity. I. Title.
  BV4597.3.B35 2011
  248.8'627—dc23

                                            2011037916

Printed in Canada
21 20 19 18 17 16 15 14   5 6 7 8 9

I f I introduced you to Leesa,[1] you'd see a talented young woman who is nice to look at, is a little shy but friendly enough, has done well in school, and is obviously good at whatever she does.

There's also a lot you wouldn't see. Leesa hasn't worn short sleeves for a couple of years. She never puts on a bathing suit. If she did she would reveal a line of scars, perfectly straight and parallel, marching up her arms.

Leesa used to cry, blow up, or get depressed when something upset her. If people were upset with her, if they put her down or made demands, she might blame them or she might blame herself. She might try to do what they wanted or she might act like she didn't care. But none of it ever solved her problem. The pain and pressure inside didn't ease no matter what she did.

Now if something upsets Leesa, others won't see it. She deals with it by going to her room and cutting herself. The blood flowing down her arm brings relief. Leesa feels like she can breathe again. She is calm; the blood makes her feel like the pain is draining from her body.

Leesa knows others think it's abnormal to get relief by cutting, but it does bring release when nothing else seems to help. She reasons, *Why would I give it up when nothing else works?* In her heart, however, she knows this doesn't work either. She now has to cut deeper and deeper, more and more frequently.

Cry Out to God

Many people feel like Leesa. You might be one of them. Maybe it's not hard to understand how you turned to cutting. But it's harder to figure out what to do when you get less and less out of doing something more and more. What happens when you can't get relief anymore? What will you do when the next stressful situation comes along and your best plan no longer works? You're out of ideas.

In your most honest moments, you know it's more than that. Cutting not only doesn't help the way it used to, it's taken on a life of its own. It used to be your safety valve, but now the cutting makes its own demands on you. You feel like you *have* to do it—you don't have a choice. You started cutting because you liked to feel in control, but now, more and more, it feels like cutting is controlling you. It's running things in a lot of ways, and it's not going in a good direction. You need help you can't give yourself, both with the cutting and with the problems you originally thought cutting would solve.

God offers you an alternative to dependence on cutting. As a cutter you have to solve all your own problems without anyone knowing how you do it. But God already knows all about it, and he knows the needs and struggles of your heart. The Lord longs to show pity and mercy to those who struggle. He is close to the brokenhearted, and *he* binds up their wounds. As you read this, ask the Lord to do that for you. Because God's love compelled him to send his Son to suffer and die for us, his love is strong enough to spill out on every soul who looks to him. And since his power was great enough to raise Christ from the dead, his power is great enough to liberate you from bondage to cutting.

Through Christ's blood, God brings people near who used to be alone. He brings people near who used to be excluded; he comes near to people without hope, people like you. Ask God to show himself to you—cry out to him.

Precious to Him

Psalm 72:12–13 tells us that God will "deliver the needy who cry out, the afflicted who have no one to help. He will take pity on the weak and needy . . . ." These are comforting truths by themselves, but the passage continues with something even more comforting: "He will rescue them from oppression and violence, for precious is their blood in his sight" (Psalm 72:14).

Did you notice that last part? Your *blood* is precious in God's sight. When you've locked yourself in your room and raised blood in order to feel calm, God has been there and your blood is precious to him. When you've reopened wounds to get relief, God has been there and your blood is precious to him. When you've needed the sight of your blood to prove you're in control, God has been there and your blood is precious to him.

Blood Is Powerful

Blood is powerful. You've been using the sight of your blood as a high-powered tool to alleviate your pain, your alienation, your aloneness, your self-loathing, and your guilt. But as you've come to recognize, your cutting doesn't solve the issues at war within your soul. Cutting only offers temporary relief—a relief that is quickly destroyed by more pain, more anxiety, more sadness, more guilt, and more desperation.

Spilling out our own blood in an attempt to find relief falls far short of the image God created us to reflect: his image. God is glorious—splendid, magnificent, radiant, holy, and altogether wonderful. And God created us to reflect his glory (Genesis 1; 1 Corinthians 10:31). We all fall short of this.

Remember, in Psalm 72 God says he will take pity on the weak and needy. Even though we've failed to reflect God's glory, even though we've looked to our own blood to control the pain and provide relief, God is willing to show us pity. His pity is shown to us in the death of his Son, who suffered and bled so we could receive a pardon for our sins and begin to reflect the glory we were designed to radiate. The blood you spill can never permanently provide relief or atone for your sins, but the blood Christ spilled for you can offer hope even beyond relief.

If you tend to think about Jesus in narrow, "religious" terms that don't overlap much with the problems in your life, take a few minutes to consider him in another light. Jesus left heaven to come to earth and fix all the things that had gone wrong since its creation. That includes the things that have hurt and damaged you. It also includes the wrong and damaging ways you have responded.

Jesus understands your struggles far more than you know. He is "a man of sorrows, and familiar with suffering" (Isaiah 53:3). He entered into the suffering of this world for our sake. He understands the broken, sinful relationships and situations that have led you to seek relief in your private world of self-injury. But he also knows why that hasn't worked for you—the inner workings of your heart are broken and sinful too. Your efforts to find relief from the pain and evil of life are also tainted with sin and brokenness. That's why your efforts to find relief are so often followed by more pain, more anxiety, more sadness, more guilt, and more desperation. Sometimes you even cut yourself to punish yourself for cutting yourself!

You need help from outside yourself. And you need help not only to deal with yourself and other people, but also to restore the relationship with God you were originally created to enjoy. That's been broken too. It's the reason everything else has gone so desperately wrong.

Jesus died on the cross to break sin's hold on each of us. He took the punishment our sins deserved and defeated the power of evil over us. The barrier between us and God has been removed. Jesus offers forgiveness for everything we have ever done wrong. He gives us a new start, with a new heart that can trust God, a new relationship with God and identity as his child, and a new purpose in life—to know God, to follow him, and to bring him joy and honor. Second Corinthians 5:17 puts it this way: "If anyone is in Christ, he is a new creation; the old has gone, the new has come!"

Christ's blood is powerful enough to rescue us from our sins *and* our efforts to rescue ourselves. It's powerful enough to free us to live for the God who knows us completely yet loves us perfectly. Have you cried out to Jesus for his forgiveness and help? Are you ready to trust in his blood instead of your own? Through Christ's blood you can leave your hidden world and allow Jesus to become your relief, satisfaction, savior, comforter, protector, and hope.

The loneliness, guilt, confusion, and powerlessness you've experienced have kept you in a dark place. But when God rescues you through Christ, you can begin to walk in the light because you're walking with Christ, and he *is* the Light. First John 1:7 says, "If we walk in the light, as he is in the light, we have fellowship with one another, and the blood of Jesus, his Son, purifies us from all sin."

Notice that walking in the light brings us into "fellowship"—relationship—with God and with others. The alienation you've felt from your parents, your peers, your teachers, your bosses, and from God has a remedy: trust in Jesus' blood, not your own. Blood is most powerful when it's Christ's blood.

Help from God

Trusting in what Jesus has done for you means you can now approach God with a boldness you didn't have in the past. With Jesus as your Brother and God as your Father, you can be confident when you ask for the help you need. Remember, God says he will deliver the needy who cry out for help. This is your time of need, so ask!

The thing to remember is that God's help comes in various forms. If you expect it to come in only one way, you may be confused and discouraged if his response doesn't meet your expectations. But there is no question that God wants to help you stop cutting and leave the world of self-injury for a very different life that is built around him. Let's consider three ways God provides help.

1. *God provides help by changing our circumstances.*
Sometimes God helps us by changing our situation so that our circumstances get better. This

happened when Jesus healed the sick, the crippled, and the blind while he was on earth.

Sometimes this help comes without any effort on our part. At other times, we need to take some sort of action. For example, in Matthew 8 when Christ healed the leper, the cure was immediate. No action was required of the leper. But in Luke 17 the ten lepers were told to go and show themselves to the priest. Their healing occurred as they followed Christ's instructions. So when we ask for help, we should always search God's Word to see if he's given any instructions we should follow.

We might be waiting for God to remove from our lives the circumstances and relationships that stress us out and make us want to cut. In some cases God does that. At other times God wants us to participate in changing those circumstances and relationships. We'll look more closely at that later.

2. God provides help by changing our desires.

Sometimes the things we want would choke out our desire for God if he gave them to us (Mark 4:19). In such cases, God may deny our request in order to give us something much better—himself.

God knows we can be corrupted by deceptive desires (Ephesians 4:22). We can fail to see where our desires would lead us and the damage they would do. After spending time in the world of self-injury, you can probably see many ways that has happened to you. God doesn't want us to hold onto the desires we had before we knew him (1 Peter 1:14). He wants better things for us—the "good and perfect gift[s]" he gives (James 1:17). Understanding this is meant to deepen our desire to get close to God so we can say as the psalmist did, "Earth has nothing I desire besides you" (Psalm 73:25).

Why is this helpful when we are trying to leave self-injury behind? Because when God is what is most important to us, we aren't devastated if things around us fall apart. We are secure in him and his love for us. God is the strength of our hearts and he's our portion forever (Psalm 73:26). He enables us to keep going even in tough times because our identity and our security are not determined by people or circumstances. Instead, what keeps us going is the fact that we are committed to God, and he is committed to us. As we look to him and follow his commands they give light to our eyes and joy to our heart (Psalm 19:7–8).

3. *God provides help by enabling us to persevere in the midst of a trial.*

This kind of help isn't always the kind of help we want, but it's often the kind of help God knows we need most. There are a lot of reasons for this. For one thing our view of suffering is often very different from God's. No doubt that is part of the reason you've injured yourself in the past—suffering is something you want to avoid. But in James 1:2 we're encouraged to "consider it pure joy . . . whenever [we] face trials of many kinds." Why would we rejoice when bad things happen instead of retreating to comfort ourselves?

Rejoice because God is making us into people who are not controlled by fear or the actions of others. Nor does he want us to be limited by what we can do in our own strength. God is enabling us to leave that behind so we can love and trust him more and experience his love and faithfulness. When our faith is tested by the trials of difficult circumstances and relationships, God's purpose is to strengthen our faith so we can trust and follow him for the long haul. James says that "the testing of [our] faith develops perseverance. Perseverance must finish its work so that [we] may be mature and complete, not lacking anything" (James 1:3–4). Becoming mature means becoming more and more like Christ (Ephesians 4:13) and trapped less and less in a world of fear, unbelief, and self-injury. If trials are God's tool to make that happen, joy is possible when we face them.

Obstacles

When you ask God to help you, you can trust that the help he gives is intended to free you from sin so that you become more like Jesus. This is hope! But as you ask for help you will probably encounter some internal obstacles that oppose what God is doing.

The first obstacle is your tendency to *trust in yourself* and seek control in the hard times. When you cut, you wanted to handle everything on your own. But if you rely on yourself, you won't be trusting God; you'll return to feeling alone, and cutting will seem appealing again. Ask God to remind you what a dead end that way of life has been. On the other hand, when you trust in God instead of yourself, you can expect to see the following promises unfold in your life:

- You'll be stable, safe, and strong—not nervous, insecure, and anxious (Psalm 9:10).
- You'll have joy, peace, and hope (Romans 15:13).
- You'll be surrounded by the Lord's unfailing love (Psalm 32:10).

- You won't be dismayed (Isaiah 28:16).
- You'll be blessed (Psalm 84:12).
- You'll have help. The Lord will be your strength and protector (Psalm 28:7).
- You'll be radiant. You won't be covered with shame (Psalm 34:5).

The Lord never forsakes those who seek him so trust him; don't trust in yourself. When you are tempted to go back to your old ways of handling life, ask God for help and he will give it to you.

The second obstacle involves the *deceitful desires* that so easily control your heart. Sometimes the things we want or think we need take on a life of their own and end up ruling us. That's what happens with cutting. What desires might rule your heart and tempt you to cut? Your desire might be control or power. You might want a life without problems. You might crave the approval of others, wanting to be well-liked and accepted.

When we believe that these things are worth more than the Lord, we will be tempted to cut if we don't get them. When we believe these desires will make us happy, we will cling to them rather than to Jesus. The desire to cut is always connected to something we want more than God but aren't getting. Ask yourself, *When I cut, what is it I want?* When something besides Jesus has dazzled you, admit it. Ask for grace and forgiveness and for a heart that wants what God wants to give you.

If we cling to cutting, it's a sign that we don't believe God is willing or able to deliver us from it. Clinging to cutting causes us to function as though we are orphans—without God as our Father and Jesus as our Brother—without anyone to take pity on us. Don't believe it! Ask God to help you trust his good plan for you and to desire nothing on earth besides him.

Combating Lies with Truth

As you seek to hold on to Jesus, put off deceitful desires, and live by the truth, let's consider some lies that may have deceived you and the emotions they produce. Then let's look at what is true and the responses the truth produces.

Lie #1: There is no solution. I'm a lost cause.

Emotions produced by this lie: hopelessness and depression.

Truth: God says he is a God of hope. He says that if you trust in him, you can overflow with hope. God says, "Those who hope in me *will not* be disappointed" (Isaiah 49:23, emphasis added).

Why not? Because God "plans to prosper you and not to harm you"; he "plans to give you hope and a future" (Jeremiah 29:11). Because God "heals the brokenhearted and binds up their wounds" (Psalm 147:3).

People don't bandage the wounds of things that are a lost cause; they throw them out. But God "raises the poor from the dust and lifts the needy from the ash heap" (Psalm 113:7). And he doesn't stop there. "He seats them with princes," the honored elite (Psalm 113:8). God wants to replace your despair with hope, gladness, and praise. He will heal your broken heart. He will care for your wounds, and he plans to treat you like royalty.

Emotions produced by these truths: comfort and hope.

Lie #2: I must have control. I can get through this on my own. Cutting gives me control.

Emotions produced by this lie: a feeling of false power.

Truth: We can't even change the color of one hair on our head (Matthew 5:36). Control belongs to God: "The earth is the LORD's, and everything in it, the world, and all who live in it" (Psalm 24:1). You can rejoice that God is in control because he uses his power to love you. His mercies are "new every morning" (Lamentations 3:22–23). He is the champion who will never be defeated. Anyone who seeks to overpower God and control the world will ultimately fail because there is no power greater than God's.

One person wisely said, "It is good to see how powerless we are because if we don't, we will live with a distorted, unhealthy view of ourselves. We will never humbly see our need for mercy and grace. By recognizing how frail and small we really are, we can know how much we need his presence, strength, wisdom and support."[2]

Emotions produced by these truths: a feeling of dependence on the true Protector, our Almighty God; a feeling of security and safety, knowing that he protects us.

Lie #3: I must have relief. I can't continue like this.

Emotions produced by this lie: a desire to give up; edginess, intolerance, and hopelessness.

Truth: We all welcome relief, and it's perfectly acceptable to ask God for it—as long as we're willing to accept that his answer may be no and we're willing to obey him whatever his answer may be.

If God doesn't give the relief we want, we must still cling to Jesus and not fall back into self-injury. Cutting communicates that we don't think we should have to endure in situations like this. It suggests that we're only willing to trust and honor God if he gives us the circumstances we want. We need to trust Jesus. He is the Good Shepherd who will lead us by still waters and make us lie down in green pastures. Even if we walk through the valley of the shadow of death, he will comfort us. He will restore our soul and give us relief at his proper time (Psalm 23).

Emotions produced by these truths: endurance, trust, and submission.

Lie #4: I must punish myself. I hate myself.
Emotions produced by this lie: self-loathing and self-hatred.

Truth: When we sin against God, there should be loathing of it because sin made it necessary for Christ to die for us. But that should lead us to run to Jesus and repent, not wallow in our own despair. When we trust in the blood of Jesus, he cleanses us from all unrighteousness.

No amount of self-punishment can ever make up for our sin. We can't wash it away by our own efforts. If we could save ourselves there would be no need for a Savior (Matthew 5:20; Romans 10:3; Galatians 2:16, 21). According to Psalm 103 belonging to the Lord yields benefits God wants you to enjoy. These include forgiveness for all your sins. God redeems your life from the pit so you don't have to punish yourself. God "crowns you with love and compassion" (v. 4) so your heart can praise him.

Emotions produced by these truths: joy and a desire to praise God.

Putting Off the Old

When we've been enslaved to something like cutting, we need to be very intentional about leaving it behind. Ephesians 4 tells us, "You were taught, with regard to your former way of life, to put off your old self, which is being corrupted by its deceitful desires; to be made new in the attitude of your minds; and to put on the new self, created to be like God in true righteousness and holiness" (4:22–24). What are some practical ways you can embrace God's truth, reject familiar lies, and make changes to keep from running back to your old habits?

- One way may be to eliminate your use of the computer so you can't easily pull up images of self-injury or e-mail friends who share your habits.
- One way may be by changing friends, possibly even schools or jobs. Friends who are still cutting will not encourage you to cling to Jesus. Now you need to surround yourself with people who will encourage you to trust in Christ.
- One way may be to give up your privacy because you've been accustomed to cutting in private. Holding onto that place of privacy can tempt you to practice old rituals. Talk with your family and trusted friends about what this choice will mean.
- You will definitely need to get rid of everything you've used to harm yourself.

Remember, God has something much better for you. He "crowns you with love and compassion" because you are his treasured possession (Psalm 103:4).

Putting On the New

Trusting in Christ enables you to move into community with others out of a desire to serve the God who loves you (Hebrews 9:14). We are privileged to show the same love to others that Christ shows to us.

With God's help we can begin to show his mercy and compassion to others. This involves learning to be kind and patient. We reflect on God's love and train ourselves not to envy or keep a mental list of wrongs done to us. We ask God to help us put the interests of others before our own. We seek to bless those who are nasty to us, and we learn to overcome evil with good.

Instead of retreating to your room and your razor, celebrate your freedom in Christ and begin looking for ways to serve—not to gain approval, not to receive praise, not to have others view you as a success, but to reflect God's presence in your life. Perhaps that would mean doing the dishes at home each night. Perhaps it would mean tutoring a student who is having a difficult time with math. Perhaps it would mean vacuuming out your dad's truck once a week. Perhaps it would mean parking at the back of the parking lot to leave the best spaces for others.

Whatever you do, do it with the goal of glorifying God. Then you can rejoice in the grace he gives you even when no one else notices, cares, or changes the way they treat you. You can rejoice because God sees, and Christ is being seen in you.

Don't Give Up!

Change is not an overnight process. God wants you to use trials and struggles to develop perseverance, because it is by perseverance that we become mature in Christ. What we've been talking about involves hard work and continued effort, but the results are lasting.

You won't always feel like persevering but you can, by God's grace. Cry out to God and he will reach out to you. Christ endured when it got really hard, and he'll help you endure too. You are precious to him. The following action steps can help you as you go to God for the help you need.

Action Steps

1. Meditate on Psalm 72:12–14 daily for a week. To meditate means to study a passage so you can call it to mind even when you don't have a Bible with you. It also means thinking about how the passage applies to you personally. Journal your thoughts.
2. Use your Bible to look up and study two or three of these scriptures every day, then journal your responses to what you read.

Psalm 9:10	Matthew 5:20
Psalm 19:7–8	Matthew 5:29–30
Psalm 24:1	Mark 4:19
Psalm 28:7	John 8:32
Psalm 32:10	Romans 10:3
Psalm 34:4	Romans 15:13
Psalm 34:5	1 Corinthians 10:18
Psalm 34:18	Galatians 2:16, 21
Psalm 56:3	Ephesians 4:13
Psalm 73:25–26	Ephesians 4:22
Psalm 84:12	Ephesians 5:1
Psalm 113:7–8	Hebrews 9:14
Psalm 147:3	James 1:2–4
Isaiah 28:16	James 1:17
Isaiah 49:23	1 Peter 1:14
Jeremiah 29:11	

3. Keep a record of the times you cried out to God and trusted in Christ's blood rather than cutting.
4. Read 1 John 1:7. Make a list of steps you will take to begin walking in the light.
5. What would reflecting God's glory look like in your life? How would it be reflected in your thinking, your desires, your communication with God, and your interaction with others?

6. Make note cards to remind yourself of what is true. Review your note cards fifteen times every day so the truth is regularly on your mind.

7. Ask a biblical counselor or a wise older believer to pray for you and support you through this process of change. Ask that person to read this booklet with you and interact with you about it. Be open about what your dark place has been like, and tell that person how you want to walk in the light.

Endnotes

1. Leesa represents a composite of women who cut themselves.

2. Wayne Mack and Joshua Mack, *The Fear Factor* (Tulsa: Hensley Publishing, 2003), 157.

Simple, Quick, Biblical

Advice on Complicated Counseling Issues
for Pastors, Counselors, and Individuals

MINIBOOK
CATEGORIES

- Personal Change
- Marriage & Parenting
- Medical & Psychiatric Issues

- Women's Issues
- Singles
- Military

USE YOURSELF | GIVE TO A FRIEND | DISPLAY IN YOUR CHURCH OR MINIS

Go to **www.newgrowthpress.com** or call **336.378.7775**
purchase individual minibooks or the entire collection.
Durable acrylic display stands are also available to house
the minibook collection.